# The Q

## *Rome*

## William Shakespeare

Copyright © 2017 Esse Publishing Limited

First published in 2016 by:
The Quotation Bank
Esse Publishing Limited

10 9 8 7 6 5 4 3

A CIP catalogue record for this book is available from the British Library.
ISBN 978-0-9956086-1-0

All enquiries to: contact@thequotationbank.co.uk

Printed and bound by Target Print Limited, Broad Lane, Cottenham, Cambridge CB24 8SW.

www.thequotationbank.co.uk

# Introduction

## Quotations

## Revision and Essay Planning

Welcome to The Quotation Bank, the comprehensive guide to all the key quotations you need to succeed in your exams.

Whilst you may have read the play, watched a production, understood the plot and have a strong grasp of context, the vast majority of marks awarded in your GCSE are for the ability to write a focused essay, full of quotations, and most importantly, quotations that you then analyse.

I think we all agree it is **analysis** that is the tricky part – and that is why we are here to help!

**The Quotation Bank** takes 25 of the most important quotations from the text, interprets them, analyses them, highlights literary techniques Shakespeare has used, puts them in context, and suggests which quotations you might use in which essays.

At the end of **The Quotation Bank** we have put together a sample answer, essay plans and great revision exercises to help you prepare for your exam. We have also included a detailed glossary to make sure you completely understand what certain literary terms actually mean!

## English Literature 9-1: What are examiners looking for?

**All GCSE Exam Boards mark your exams using the same Assessment Objectives (AOs) – around 80% of your mark across the English Literature GCSE will be awarded for A01 and A02.**

| | |
|---|---|
| **A01** | Read, understand and respond to texts. Students should be able to: <br> • Maintain a critical style and develop an *informed personal response* <br> • Use textual references, *including quotations*, to support and illustrate *interpretations*. |
| **A02** | Analyse the *Language, Form and Structure* used by a writer to *create meanings and effects*, using *relevant subject terminology* where appropriate. |

Basically, **AO1** is the ability to answer the question set, showing a good knowledge of the text, and using quotations to back up ideas and interpretations.

**AO2** is the ability to analyse these quotations, as well as the literary techniques the writer uses, and to show you understand the effect of these on the audience.

We will also highlight elements of **AO3** – the context in which the play is set.

## How The Quotation Bank can help you in your exams.

**The Quotation Bank is designed to make sure that every point you make in an essay clearly fulfils the Assessment Objectives an examiner will be using when marking your work.**

**Every quotation comes with the following detailed material:**

Interpretation: The interpretation of each quotation allows you to fulfil **AO1**, responding to the text and giving an informed personal response.

Techniques: Using subject-specific terminology correctly (in this case, the literary devices used by Shakespeare) is a key part of **AO2**.

Analysis: We have provided as much analysis (**AO2**) as possible. It is a great idea to analyse the quotation in detail – you need to do more than just say what it means, but also what effect the language, form and structure has on the audience.

Use in essays on… Your answer needs to be focused to fulfil **AO1**. This section helps you choose relevant quotations and link them together for a stronger essay.

## How to use The Quotation Bank.

Many students spend time learning quotations by heart.

This is an excellent idea, but they often forget what they are meant to do with those quotations once they get into the exam!

By using **The Quotation Bank**, not only will you have a huge number of quotations to use in your essays, you will also have ideas on what to say about them, how to analyse them, how to link them together, and what questions to use them for.

For GCSE essay questions, these quotations can form the basis of your answer, making sure every point comes **directly from the text (AO1)** and allowing you to **analyse language, form and structure (AO2)**. We also highlight where you can easily and effectively include **context (AO3)**.

For GCSE questions that give you an extract to analyse, the quotations in **The Quotation Bank** are excellent not only for revising the skills of **analysis (AO2)**, but also for showing **wider understanding of the text (AO1)**.

**The Prologue:**
> CHORUS: "The fearful passage of their death-mark'd love."

**Interpretation:** Romeo and Juliet are on a pre-determined journey that will end in death – even their love will not overcome this.

**Techniques:** Juxtaposition; Imagery.

**Analysis:**

- The lovers' lives are described using the image of a "passage" – a pre-determined route with only one possible way out, as if their destiny was already set. Many of Shakespeare's audience would have had a firm belief in fate.
- The use of the adjective "fearful" emphasises the harm and pain that <u>will</u> come to Romeo and Juliet, both emotionally and physically.
- We are introduced to the constant battle between love and hate – the juxtaposition of "death-mark'd love" suggests love has already been tainted and stained. Shakespeare makes it explicit – they will die, and the audience therefore have a stronger awareness of death every time it appears in the play.

**Use in essays on…**Love and Hate; Death; Fate.

**Act One Scene One:**
>    ROMEO: "Here's much to do with hate, but more with love:/Why then, O
>                   brawling love, O loving hate."

**Interpretation:** Love and hate are frequently linked throughout the play, an indication of the constant conflict between them.

**Techniques:** Sentence structure; Oxymoron.

**Analysis:**
- Whilst Romeo knows the feud is about hate, the sentence structure stresses "more with love" – Romeo believes that love of your family (particularly in a time when family, and family honour, were key parts of society) will defeat hate.
- The oxymoron of "brawling love" highlights the conflict and tension in the play, but also the violence that becomes more and more frequent.
- The contrast of "loving hate" suggests powerful, passionate feelings, but also how quickly one emotion can turn into another.

**Use in essays on…**Conflict; Love and Hate; Violence; The Feud; Honour.

**Act One Scene Two:**

    **CAPULET:** "Behold this night/Earth-treading stars that make dark heaven light."

**Interpretation:** An ironic statement from Lord Capulet – Romeo and Juliet are indeed "stars" who, whilst currently "earth-treading", will soon make "heaven light".

**Techniques:** Irony; Juxtaposition; Metaphor.

**Analysis:**

- The metaphor "Earth-treading stars" presents Romeo and Juliet as heavenly and too pure for this violent, imperfect earth.
- The idea that Romeo and Juliet are stars suggests they bring light and brightness to the world, which they do at the end of the play when Montague and Capulet end the feud and turn them into gold statues.
- Even heaven, a place Shakespeare's audience would view as perfect and spiritual, is "dark" until Romeo and Juliet give it light.

**Use in essays on…**Religion; Conflict; Death.

**Act One Scene Four:**
> ROMEO: "He that hath the steerage of my course/Direct my sail."

**Interpretation:** Is this Romeo taking control of his life, actively choosing to attend the party, or has he fallen victim to the inevitability of fate?

**Techniques:** Personification; Imagery.

**Analysis:**
- The use of the pronoun "he" personifies fate. Romeo's destiny is in the hands of a living, thinking being who makes his decisions for him. Shakespeare's audiences were more likely to believe in fate than modern audiences.
- The imagery of life being a boat journey is highly appropriate – like the sea it can be rough, dangerous and entirely unpredictable. "Steerage" and "direct" suggest Romeo is being manoeuvred down a "course" – his path has already been determined by fate.
- There is an immature tone to this statement – is Romeo trying to impress Mercutio and his friends?

**Use in essays on…** Fate; Romeo; Religion; Youth.

**Act One Scene Five:**
  TYBALT: "This intrusion shall,/Now seeming sweet, convert to bitt'rest gall."

**Interpretation:** The audience is about to observe one of Shakespeare's most romantic scenes, the first meeting of Romeo and Juliet. However, before we do, the audience watch Tybalt promise to poison Romeo's future happiness.

**Techniques:** Sibilance; Juxtaposition.

**Analysis:**
- There is a sense of inevitability about the pain that is to come – the definitive "shall" makes future troubles seem certain.
- The sibilance in "seeming sweet" adds a swiftness to the sentence – any sweetness will quickly disappear, and all that will be left is the poisonous "gall" that Tybalt promises.
- The adjective "bitt'rest" implies Tybalt doesn't simply want to harm Romeo, he wants to inflict complete and total pain on him.

**Use in essays on…** Tybalt; Love and Hate; Fate; The Feud; Honour.

**Act Two Scene Two:**
    ROMEO: "Juliet is the sun./Arise, fair sun, and kill the envious moon."

**Interpretation:** Juliet is more than just a beautiful woman but also a powerful sun, bright and magnificent. The audience would compare the simple beauty of this metaphor to the jumbled poetry Romeo created for Rosaline.

**Techniques:** Metaphor; Juxtaposition.

**Analysis:**
- The metaphor of "the sun" gives Juliet all the sun's positive associations – she brings life, warmth and light to the world (Juliet is frequently associated with light throughout the play).
- There is a juxtaposition between the "fair" sun and the "envious" moon. Again, as with all conflict in the play, the relationship between the sun and moon ends in violence and death as Romeo instructs the sun to "kill" the moon.
- The irony here is that at the end of the play, Juliet does not "arise", but it is instead she who is killed.

**Use in essays on…**Juliet; Love and Hate; Conflict.

**Act Two Scene Two:**
**JULIET:** "I have no joy of this contract tonight,/It is too rash, too unadvised, too sudden,/Too like the lightning."

**Interpretation:** Romeo and Juliet's love is incredibly intense, but Juliet is aware of the problems that will arise from acting too quickly, reminding the audience of the family situation behind this relationship.

**Techniques:** Repetition; Simile.

**Analysis:**
- The repetition of the adverb "too" highlights Romeo and Juliet's fate – the hatred of the feud and the world in general is too intense for them to survive.
- The adjectives "rash", "unadvised" and "sudden" may seem like the characteristics of young, romantic love, but Shakespeare's audience may have seen marriage as far more of a contract than anything to do with love.
- The simile "like the lightning" suggests both a powerful, passionate and destructive feeling, and also how quickly one emotion can turn into another.

**Use in essays on…**Love; Youth; Marriage.

**Act Two Scene Three:**
  **FRIAR: "Within the infant rind of this weak flower/Poison hath residence, and medicine power."**

**Interpretation:** The Friar highlights that in nature things often contain both the power to harm and the power to heal.

**Techniques:** Language; Symbolism; Juxtaposition.

**Analysis:**
- The use of "infant" and "weak" are both symbolic of Romeo and Juliet – they are essentially young children, vulnerable in a world that expects them to grow up quickly.
- The personification of poison which "hath residence" suggests the harmful nature of the plant is almost lying in wait, hidden in something seemingly sweet.
- The sentence structure stresses that medicine has "power" – we have the ability to heal, as we see at the very end of the play.

**Use in essays on…**Conflict; Love and Hate; The Friar.

**Act Two Scene Three:**
 **FRIAR: "For this alliance may so happy prove/To turn your households' rancour to pure love."**

**Interpretation:** The Friar, whilst wary that this marriage is very sudden, sees the purity of Romeo and Juliet's love and the potential to end the feud.

**Techniques:** Language; Juxtaposition.

**Analysis:**
- The Friar is being calculating here – his main aim is "alliance", suggesting two families coming together. It has a political tone rather than a romantic one.
- However, the use of "may" creates tension – there is no certainty this will work.
- There is a contrast between two conflicting ideas. On one side, the "pure love" of Romeo and Juliet may seem powerful to a modern audience. However, to a Shakespearean audience, the importance of loyalty to "your households' rancour" may be more important than true love.

**Use in essays on…**Family; Honour; Love; The Friar; The Feud.

**Act Two Scene Six:**
 **ROMEO:** "Then love-devouring Death do what he dare,/It is enough I may but call her mine."

**Interpretation:** Romeo believes that his love for Juliet is above earthly feelings. With such a strong belief in the afterlife, he believes not even death will separate them.

**Techniques:** Personification; Alliteration; Dramatic irony.

**Analysis:**
- The alliteration of the "d" sound is strong and powerful – it emphasises Romeo's challenge to Death.
- The dramatic irony is particularly painful here – just minutes before their marriage, Romeo foolishly challenges death, and the audience knows that death wins.
- The image of "love-devouring" suggests love is fragile, vulnerable and delicate, whilst "devouring" has associations with animalistic, beast like behaviour.

**Use in essays on…**Fate; Death; Marriage.

**Act Three Scene One:**
 **ROMEO:** "Away to heaven, respective lenity,/And fire-eyed fury be my conduct now."

**Interpretation:** For the first time, Romeo sees hate as more powerful and appealing than love. Like most characters in the play, only violence can redeem his honour.

**Techniques:** Alliteration; Personification.

**Analysis:**

- The repetition of the "f" sound is violent and aggressive, foreshadowing the scene ahead. Much of Shakespeare's audience would see this behaviour as the correct, 'masculine' way of behaving.
- The personification of "fury" being "fire-eyed" depicts an image of someone not being able to see clearly. Romeo is blinded by fire, something deadly and destructive, and his wish to avenge Mercutio's death is all consuming.
- Yet again, Romeo has placed his fate in the hands of something else. The phrase "be my conduct" once again suggests he is not making his own decisions.

**Use in essays on…**Fate; Violence; Death; Romeo.

**Act Three Scene One:**

**ROMEO: "O, I am fortune's fool."**

**Interpretation:** Romeo has repeatedly given over his destiny to Fate – here he realises that it is simply playing with him, and he is nothing but a fool to believe it would treat him kindly.

**Techniques:** Alliteration; Personification.

**Analysis:**

- Much like when he referenced "fire-eyed fury", the repetition of the "f" sound is violent and aggressive, foreshadowing the acts ahead.
- The stress of the sentence falls on "fool" – the audience see Romeo not as a lover, or a vengeful friend, but as a meaningless plaything for Fate. His youth and immaturity could also be commented on here.
- The audience may well begin to question their own destinies – the definitive "I am" suggests that fate is the only thing that controls an individual's destiny.

**Use in essays on…**Fate; Romeo; Religion.

**Act Three Scene Two:**
   JULIET: "An impatient child that hath new robes/And may not wear them."

**Interpretation:** Against the violence and death in the surrounding scenes, we see a quiet, intimate scene where an individual has a sense of excitement and joy for the future.

**Techniques:** Soliloquy; Metaphor; Scene structure; Dramatic irony.

**Analysis:**
- Shakespeare structures the play to show us death in Act Three Scene One, then this loving, intimate soliloquy, then pain and suffering in Act Three Scene Three. The audience constantly sees love defeated by hate.
- The metaphor of Juliet being an "impatient child" is somewhat ironic. To many in the audience she is still a child, and it is Romeo and Juliet's impatience that causes the problems in the play.
- Again, there is a sense of dramatic irony – the idea that she has new clothes but "may not wear them" is exactly how her marriage to Romeo unfolds. She may be married, but they "may not" be able to enjoy their new life together.

**Use in essays on…**Love; Youth; Marriage; Juliet.

**Act Three Scene Five:**
   JULIET: "It is the lark that sings so out of tune,/Straining harsh discords and
   unpleasing sharps."

**Interpretation:** Romeo and Juliet have spent the night together before he is banished.
The normally beautiful lark, who signals the morning with its song, is now a painful
reminder of what the future holds.

**Techniques:** Symbolism; Sibilance; Language.

**Analysis:**
- The lark is usually a bird symbolising morning joy and hope for a new day.
  Here, joy and optimism have been defeated by pain and pessimism – even
  nature has been drawn into the idea of conflict that fills the play.
- Simple language emphasises the heartbreak of the scene – "straining", "harsh"
  and "unpleasing" perfectly convey what the new day will bring for the lovers.
- The sibilance of the statement creates an unpleasant sound – much like the lark,
  Juliet's words are not what the audience want to hear.

**Use in essays on…**Conflict; Marriage; Youth.

**Act Three Scene Five:**
**CAPULET:** "And you be mine, I'll give you to my friend;/And you be not, hang, beg, starve, die in the streets."

**Interpretation:** When Juliet rejects Paris, Capulet turns against her in the most violent, hateful way imaginable, claiming she can die in the streets if she refuses to obey. In a patriarchal society, her father legally controls her.

**Techniques:** Language; Listing.

**Analysis:**

- The statement "I'll give you to my friend" contradicts Capulet's earlier view on marriage. Juliet is just an object and "give" implies Capulet owns her.
- There is venom in what Capulet says. He doesn't just simply banish her, he has a lengthy list of things he wishes to happen to her, as if to prolong her suffering. The monosyllabic words add to the violence with which they can be delivered.
- Capulet's language lowers her socially, to the level of a criminal ("hang") or vagabond ("beg, starve"). He destroys her physically, emotionally and socially.

**Use in essays on…**Marriage; Family; Violence.

**Act Four Scene One:**
> **PARIS:** "Thy face is mine, and thou hast slandered it."

**Interpretation:** Paris is trying to be a strong husband and to comfort Juliet so as to stop her crying. However, all he does is highlight patriarchal views of marriage, making Juliet more determined and defiant in her plans.

**Techniques:** Language; Dramatic irony.

**Analysis:**
- The marriage between Romeo and Juliet is a romantic partnership of people who view each other as equals in love. However, Paris uses vocabulary to do with individuals – "thy", "mine" and "thou" all imply that in marriage, Paris and Juliet would be two separate individuals, not a loving couple.
- Earlier, Romeo spoke of Juliet using beautiful poetry. Paris focuses on Juliet's external beauty, rather than her internal qualities and the value of her soul.
- This scene is full of irony. Paris believes Juliet is at church to prepare for her wedding to him. Instead, she is there with the intention to kill herself if need be.

**Use in essays on…**Marriage; Love; Paris.

**Act Four Scene One:**
> JULIET: "Come weep with me, past hope, past cure, past help."

**Interpretation:** Juliet has attended church to speak with the Friar, but she is not looking for divine intervention. Instead, she believes the situation is helpless.

**Techniques:** Tri-colon (or list of three); Repetition.

**Analysis:**
- The repetition of "past" emphasises that Juliet has lost faith and believes that all good in her life is now behind her – the future only holds negatives.
- When people are troubled, they often turn to religion ("hope"), medicine ("cure") or authority ("help"). The tri-colon highlights how none of these solutions are available to her.
- Juliet's vulnerability and youthfulness is shown when the only solution she can see is to "weep", a childish, emotional reaction emphasising the sorrow she feels.

**Use in essays on…**Juliet; Religion; The Friar; Youth.

**Act Four Scene One:**
>    JULIET: "I will do it without fear or doubt,/To live an unstained wife to my sweet love."

**Interpretation:** Juliet is bravely taking action, and for two honourable reasons – to be with the man she loves, but also to remain pure and "unstained" by not marrying Paris.

**Techniques:** Imagery; Language.

**Analysis:**

- The use of the modal verb "will" is strong and defiant – unlike Romeo, who puts his future in the hands of fate, Juliet takes control over her own destiny.
- "Fear" and "doubt" are strong, crippling emotions that overcome most characters in the play, but the audience admire Juliet for the fact she will go through with the Friar's plan "without fear or doubt".
- Even as the play descends into tragedy, the audience is reminded of Romeo and Juliet's shining goodness – "unstained" suggests purity and "sweet" suggests kindness, two elements Romeo and Juliet continue to bring to the play.

**Use in essays on…**Juliet; Fate; Death; Marriage.

**Act Four Scene Three:**
**JULIET: "My dismal scene I needs must act alone."**

**Interpretation:** Never has Juliet seemed more isolated. Just a young girl, she is about to fake her own death, and has no one to turn to in such a difficult situation – even the Nurse cannot provide protection.

**Techniques:** Symbolism; Semantic field; Language.

**Analysis:**
- Juliet uses "scene" and "act" to describe what is happening, words from the semantic field of drama. This is symbolic of the fact Romeo and Juliet have no control over their own actions; they are simply actors in a play dictated by Fate.
- Again, Juliet's isolation is made clear to the audience – the words "my", "I" and "alone" all highlight she has no one to turn to when Romeo is banished.
- The adjective "dismal" is particular painful when the audience remember that it is just days since she married Romeo – since then, the whole action of the play has been descending into tragedy.

**Use in essays on…**Juliet; Death; Family.

**Act Four Scene Five:**
   NURSE: "O woe! O woeful, woeful, woeful day! / Most lamentable day, most woeful day."

**Interpretation:** Believing Juliet to be dead, the Capulet family display their grief, but none more painfully and uncontrollably than the Nurse.

**Techniques:** Repetition; Assonance.

**Analysis:**
- The Nurse's grief is emphasised by fractured sentence structure and repetition of "woeful" and "day" – this is not elegant verse or thoughtful poetry, but raw emotion encapsulated by "woe" and "lamentable" and all their associations.
- Repetition of "O" highlights the natural, unashamed sorrow the Nurse feels – it is instinctive and human, rather than reserved or rehearsed. All of her funny stories, humorous jokes or caring advice have disappeared.
- The heavy assonance of the "o" vowel sound in "O", "woeful" and "most" creates a negative tone, mimicking the deep pain and anguish she feels.

**Use in essays on…** The Nurse; Death; Family.

**Act Five Scene One:**
>   **BALTHASAR: "Your looks are pale and wild, and do import/Some misadventure."**

**Interpretation:** As Romeo is told the news of Juliet's supposed death, he looks out of control. Balthasar fears what he may do as impending tragedy is clearly getting closer.

**Techniques:** Language; Imagery.

**Analysis:**
- "Wild" suggests Romeo is almost animalistic in his behaviour, and links closely with the previous "fire-eyed fury" that took over him in Act Three. That led to Tybalt's death – this "wild" behaviour will lead to many more.
- Balthasar's use of adjectives is key here – the use of "pale" has associations with sickness and death, and foreshadows the deaths that are to come.
- "Some misadventure" strikes fear within the audience, but is also a dramatic understatement – it is not a misadventure that is coming, but death.

**Use in essays on…**Fate; Violence; Death; Romeo.

**Act Five Scene One:**
   **ROMEO:** "O mischief, thou art swift/To enter in the thoughts of desperate men."

**Interpretation:** Romeo, having decided to kill himself and lie by Juliet's side, thinks about how quickly people turn to destructive behaviour when situations become dire.

**Techniques:** Personification; Language.

**Analysis:**

- Many elements of the play (Fate, Fortune and Death for example) have been personified, all of which seem to have evil intentions. Here, "mischief" has more playful connotations than the three above, as if it is toying with Romeo and his emotions – it seems to enjoy his pain.
- The adjective "swift" emphasises the unstoppable speed with which the tragedy is unfolding.
- Imagery of "mischief" entering "the thoughts of desperate men" gives the sense of someone being hunted and stalked, as if they are a chosen victim.

**Use in essays on…**Fate; Death; Violence.

**Act Five Scene Three:**
**ROMEO: "Thou detestable maw, thou womb of death,/Gorged with the dearest morsel of the earth."**

**Interpretation:** In Shakespeare's time, death was a frequent part of life, also linked to religion and the afterlife. Romeo chooses not to focus on Juliet in heaven, but on the horrific pain of his loss.

**Techniques:** Personification; Metaphor; Oxymoron.

**Analysis:**

- The oxymoronic metaphor "womb of death" takes the audience back to the Prologue, reminding us that Romeo and Juliet were born to die – it is their fate.
- One of the Seven Deadly Sins is Gluttony, a greedy desire to eat too much. Here Romeo personifies the tomb Juliet is buried in, usually seen as a religious resting place, and describes it as a "maw" (stomach) that "gorged" on Juliet as a "morsel", suggesting that religion has become corrupted.
- The adjective "dearest" and use of "earth" reminds us of Juliet's perfection.

**Use in essays on…**Religion; Juliet; Death.

**Act Five Scene Three:**
  **FRIAR: "A greater power than we can contradict/Hath thwarted our intents."**

**Interpretation:** The Friar, a man of God, has admitted defeated and believes they had been destined to fail as a "greater power" has decided their plan would not succeed.

**Techniques:** Personification; Language.

**Analysis:**

- It is important that the Friar delivers this line. He refers to a "greater power" rather than explicitly to God, leaving it deliberately ambiguous as to whether the Friar is referring to God or Fate as this "greater power".
- The noun "intents" has associations with positive reasons for the plan the Friar and Juliet put in place – they only intended to do good.
- "Contradict" and "thwarted" show that conflict continues to dictate the outcome of the play – even though the Friar and Juliet had good "intents", the greater power has decided to destroy them.

**Use in essays on…**Fate; Death; Religion; Conflict.

**Act Five Scene Three:**
  PRINCE: "See what a scourge is laid upon your hate,/That heaven finds means
                                    to kill your joys with love."

**Interpretation:** The Prince highlights the painful irony that the feud between Capulet and Montague didn't just lead them to lose their children, but that the sorrow was increased by making them fall in love first. It was love that led to death.

**Techniques:** Personification; Juxtaposition.

**Analysis:**
- The Prince describes the whole scenario as a "scourge" (plague), a word that could have religious connotations, as if the outcome was a plague or punishment from "heaven" for their behaviour.
- "Heaven" is a symbol of love, safety and joy. It highlights the sheer brutality of the feud that the only way heaven could end it was by killing their children.
- The play ends with the ultimate conflict – "hate" (the feud) can only be ended by taking away their "joys" (Romeo and Juliet), who are killed "with love".

**Use in essays on…**Love and Hate; Death; Conflict.

# Major Themes

| Love and Hate | Marriage | The Feud |
| Honour | Violence | Religion |
| Conflict | Family | Love |
| Youth | Death | Fate |

# Major Characters

| Romeo | Juliet | Mercutio |
| Montagues | Capulets | The Friar |
| Benvolio | Tybalt | The Prince |
| Balthasar | The Nurse | Paris |

## How to revise effectively.

One mistake people often make is to try to revise EVERYTHING!

This is clearly not possible.

Instead, once you know and understand the plot, a great idea is to pick three or four major themes, and three or four major characters, and revise these in great detail.

If, for example, you revised Juliet and Family, you will also have covered a huge amount of material to use in questions about Love, Conflict or The Feud.

Or, if you revised Honour and Violence, you would certainly have plenty of material if a question on Romeo, Tybalt or Death was set.

Use the following framework as a basis for setting *any* of your own revision questions – simply swap the theme or character to create a new essay title!

**How does Shakespeare portray the theme of _____ in *Romeo and Juliet*?**

**How does the character of _____ develop as the play progresses?**

A sample essay paragraph (top level), using ideas directly from The Quotation Bank (page 12).

### *How does Shakespeare present the character of Juliet?*

Juliet is not simply a young girl who falls in love with a boy from a rival family, but someone almost heavenly or celestial, shown frequently through Shakespeare's use of language choice and imagery. In Act Two, Scene Two, Romeo states, <u>"Juliet is the sun./Arise, fair sun, and kill the envious moon"</u>. Juliet is more than just someone with physical beauty but is also seen by Romeo as a powerful sun, bright and magnificent, made all the more obvious when the audience think back to the jumbled poetry Romeo created for Rosaline. The metaphor of <u>"the sun"</u> gives Juliet all the sun's positive associations – she brings life, warmth and light to the world (Juliet is frequently associated with light). However, Juliet may be heavenly, but she continually reminds the audience of the conflict and pain in the play. There is juxtaposition between the <u>"fair"</u> sun and the jealous moon. Again, as with all conflict in the play, the relationship between the sun and moon ends in violence and death as Romeo instructs the sun to <u>"kill"</u> the moon. The irony here is that at the end of the play, Juliet does not <u>"arise"</u>, but it is instead she who is killed.

## Potential Essay Questions

How is the idea of fate portrayed in *Romeo and Juliet*?

**Topic Sentence 1:** Fate is frequently personified as a figure that seems to take great delight in the destruction of innocence.

**Use:** Pages 18 and 28.

**Topic Sentence 2:** This is accentuated by the way fate is portrayed as always in conflict with religion.

**Use:** Pages 17 and 30.

**Topic Sentence 3:** Furthermore, fate is frequently linked with violence.

**Use:** Pages 11 and 16.

**Topic Sentence 4:** Fundamentally, fate is portrayed as unbeatable.

**Use:** Pages 7 and 10.

## How is conflict portrayed in *Romeo and Juliet*?

**Topic Sentence 1:** Conflict in Romeo and Juliet is frequently violent and aggressive, all too often ending in disturbing consequences.

**Use:** Pages 8, 11 and 17.

**Topic Sentence 2:** Conflict also occurs in seemingly loving settings, tainting what should be a pure and wholesome emotion.

**Use:** Pages 12 and 20.

**Topic Sentence 3:** Furthermore, religion and fate seem to be in constant conflict, battling to gain power over one another.

**Use:** Pages 9, 14 and 30.

**Topic Sentence 4:** Essentially, conflict frequently ends in death.

**Use:** Pages 31 and 25.

## What is the role of family in *Romeo and Juliet*?

**Topic Sentence 1:** Whilst family should be a supportive unit, ironically family is a source of frequent violence and aggression in the play.

**Use:** Pages 8 and 31.

**Topic Sentence 2:** Much of this violence stems from a concept of family honour.

**Use:** Pages 11 and 15.

**Topic Sentence 3:** However, family often provides a sense of entrapment, particularly to women.

**Use:** Pages 21 and 22.

**Topic Sentence 4:** Whatever the role of family, it provides very little support for Romeo and Juliet.

**Use:** Pages 23, 25 and 26.

How does Romeo develop throughout the play?

**Topic Sentence 1:** It is clear from the beginning of the play that Romeo is a man who frequently puts his destiny in the hands of fate.

**Use:** Pages 10 and 17.

**Topic Sentence 2:** He develops into a man who wishes to take back control, but when he tries to it always ends tragically.

**Use:** Pages 18 and 28

**Topic Sentence 3:** In essence, Romeo is a romantic young man.

**Use:** Pages 12, 15 and 16

**Topic Sentence 4:** However, as the play develops we see that his focus on love will eventually succumb to hate and death.

**Use:** Pages 7 and 27.

## Suggested Revision Activities

Major character and themes – Take any of the major characters and themes (see page 32 for a list) and group together quotations in sets of 2 or 3 to answer the following question: "How does the theme/character develop as the play goes on?"

You should try to get 4 sets of quotations, giving you 8-12 overall.

A great cover and repeat exercise – Cover the whole page, apart from the quotation at the top. Can you now fill in the four sections in your exercise book without looking – Interpretations, Techniques, Analysis, Use in essays on…?

This also works really well as a revision activity with a friend – cover the whole card, apart from the quotation at the top. If you read out the quotation, can they tell you the four sections without looking – Interpretations, Techniques, Analysis, Use in essays on…?

"The Development Game" – **Pick any quotation at random from The Quotation Bank and use it to create an essay question, and then create a focused topic sentence to start the essay. Next, find another appropriate quotation to develop your idea even further.**

"The Contrast Game" – **Follow the same rules as The Development Game, but instead of finding a quotation to support your idea, find a quotation that can be used to start a counter-argument.**

Your very own Quotation Bank! **Using the same headings and format as The Quotation Bank, find 10 more quotations from throughout the text (select them from many different sections of the text to help develop whole text knowledge) and create your own revision cards.**

Essay writing – **They aren't always fun, but writing essays is great revision. Choose a practice question and then try taking three quotations and writing out a perfect paragraph, making sure you add connectives, technical vocabulary and sophisticated language.**

## Glossary

**Alliteration** – Repetition of the same consonant or sound at the beginning of a number of words in a sentence: "love-devouring Death do what he dare" creates a strong, powerful "d" sound, as if Romeo is challenging Death.

**Assonance** – Repetition of the vowel sound: "O woe! O woeful" creates a negative tone, mimicking the deep pain and anguish the Nurse feels at Juliet's death.

**Dramatic Irony** – When the audience knows something the characters don't: when Romeo says "Death do what he dare" the audience feel increased pain as we know they will die.

**Imagery** – Figurative language that appeals to the senses of the audience: "unstained wife" creates an image of a pure, untainted woman.

**Juxtaposition** – Two ideas, images or words placed next to each other to create a contrasting effect: "poison" and "medicine" are used together to highlight the ability to kill and the ability to cure within the same situation.

**Language** – The vocabulary chosen to create effect.

**Metaphor** – A word or phrase used to describe something else so that the first idea takes on the associations of the second: "Earth treading stars" links Romeo and Juliet to the heavens.

**Oxymoron** – A figure of speech where apparently contradictory terms appear together: "O brawling love" links the ideas of violence and love.

**Personification** – A non-human object or concept takes on human qualities to make its presence more vivid to the audience: "I am fortune's fool" suggests Romeo has been deceived by an intelligent, manipulative being.

**Repetition** – When a word, phrase or idea is repeated to reinforce it: "woeful" is repeated by the Nurse to emphasise her anguish at Juliet's death.

**Semantic Field** – A group of words used together from the same topic area: "scene" and "act" both come from the genre of theatre, suggesting Romeo and Juliet are simply playing a part in a play directed by fate.

**Sentence Structure** – The way the writer has ordered the words in a sentence to create a certain effect: "much to do with hate, but more with love" ends with love, stressing love should defeat hate.

**Sibilance** – A variation on alliteration, usually of the 's' sound, that creates a hissing sound: "this intrusion shall,/Now seeming sweet" accentuates the hatred of Tybalt's threat.

**Simile** – A comparison of one thing with something of a different kind, used to make a description more vivid: "too like the lightning" emphasises the speed with which Romeo and Juliet have fallen in love.

**Soliloquy** – A speech when a character talks to themselves: Juliet's soliloquy waiting for Romeo to arrive accentuates how alone she will become.

**Symbolism** – The use of a symbol to represent an idea: the flower with poison and medicine shows the dual nature of man.

**Tri-colon** – A list of three words or phrases for effect: "past hope, past cure, past help" suggests religion, medicine or support are all useless in Juliet's situation.